H

H

A Jou   g   ..ine

A 100-mile walk to and
along the Roman frontier

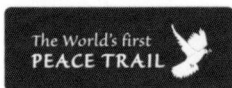

Mark Richards

Part 1: Ravenglass to Penrith
75km (47 miles)

First published in 2017 by
PathMaster
An imprint of J R Nicholls
Denby Dale HD8 8RT

ISBN: 978-1-911347-50-7

Printed and bound in Great Britain by
CPI Group (UK) Ltd, Croydon CR0 4YY

Disclaimer: Whilst every care and effort has been taken in the preparation of this book, the reader should be aware that walking can be a dangerous activity and conditions can be variable. Therefore, neither J R Nicholls Publishing nor the Author accept liability for damage of any nature (including damage to property, personal injury or death) arising directly or indirectly from the information in this book.

HADRIAN'S HIGH WAY

Carlisle

This 100-mile walk to Vindolanda can efficiently be broken at Penrith creating two remarkable and hugely scenic short-week walking holidays.

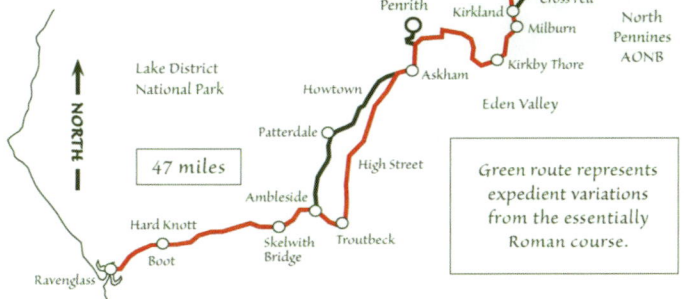

Great Chesters
Carvoran
Greenhead
Blenkinsopp Castle
Housesteads
Vindolanda
Bardon Mill
Slaggyford
Whitley Castle
Alston
Hartside Pass
Garrigill
55 miles
Penrith
Kirkland
Cross Fell
Milburn
North Pennines AONB
Askham
Kirkby Thore
Lake District National Park
Howtown
Eden Valley
Patterdale
High Street
47 miles
Ambleside
Hard Knott
Skelwith Bridge
Troutbeck
Boot
Ravenglass

NORTH

Green route represents expedient variations from the essentially Roman course.

Recommended maps:

Part 1 Ravenglass to Penrith
Ordnance Survey Explorer Series   OL5, OL6 & OL7

Part 2 Penrith to Vindolanda
Ordnance Survey Explorer Series   OL5, OL19, OL31 & OL43

The Countryside Code

Be safe - plan ahead and follow any signs

Leave gates and property as you find them

Protect plants and animals, and take your litter home

Keep dogs under close control

Consider other people

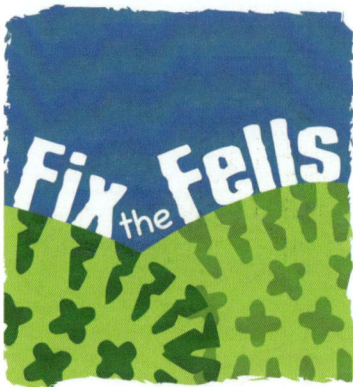

Fix the Fells is a collaborative partnership programme between the National Trust, the Lake District National Park, Nurture Lakeland, Friends of the Lake District, Natural England and Cumbria County Council. The aim of the Fix the Fells partnership is to protect the spectacular Lakeland fells from erosion and damage by repairing and maintaining the upland paths of the Lake District. For more information, visit fixthefells.co.uk.

Publisher's note in support of Fix the Fells

We are extremely proud to be the publisher of the guide books for Mark Richards' great new long distance trails. New routes for outdoor enthusiasts will hopefully provide a positive impact on the towns and villages of the Lake District, taking the enthusiastic walker into parts of the region not usually on the tourist trail, as well as the more familiar areas. We hope this has a beneficial impact on the communities alongside these routes.

However, whilst there is hopefully a positive impact to the community we are keenly aware that there is the potential for a negative impact on the very fells and footpaths that facilitate the routes. A combination of millions of pairs of walking boots, the weather and gradient means erosion is a constant problem. To this end, we have committed to donating a proportion of the revenue from the sale of each guide to 'Fix the Fells'.

We are very proud to support their work. If you would like to find out more, and maybe give a donation of your own or even volunteer to help, you can find further details about their work at www.fixthefells.co.uk.

We hope you enjoy these new guides.

DEDICATION

To David Breeze

Reaching back some quarter of a century to when I first became enthralled by Hadrian's Wall, David's scholarship has been a shining beacon of wisdom for me. His treaties have been valued companions and trusted references. Hence I consider it a great honour to be able to offer my grateful thanks to him for his support in recent years and, very specifically, with the creation of this guide. Together we share the hope that the route will open walkers' eyes to the wider Roman influence in the landscape, and to some degree relieve some of the intense pressure on the archaeology caused by the concentration of boots on Hadrian's Wall Path National Trail.

ACKNOWLEDGEMENTS

First and foremost my darling wife Helen, an ever-sure support and, with this route research, my taxi too! Peter Savin, who walked the route with me, his keen eyes helping me scrutinise the landscape and in particular look closer at historic detail. Dawn McMullan and Rachael Thompson, who joined me in traversing Muncaster Fell and cheered me on my way at the start. Dayna Hadwen appropriately shared a day on the Maiden Way, while Malcolm Redman sampled the valley stretch from Brougham to Kirkby Thore. Friendships are strengthened on a good country walk, especially one as rich in history as this remarkable journey. I would also like to extend my thanks to Chris Woodley-Stewart, Director of the North Pennines AONB, and Peter Frost-Pennington of Muncaster Castle for their all-important local advice, while not forgetting the enthusiasm shown by Elaine Edgar of Castle Nook Farm. Finally, my thanks to David McGlade who, for 22 years, has been a determined bulwark and the constant voice of calm reason in his role of Hadrian's Wall Path National Trail Officer.

Foreword

The *Convention concerning the Protection of the World Cultural and Natural Heritage* was adopted by UNESCO's General Conference in 1972. Its aim is to encourage the identification, protection and preservation of cultural and natural heritage around the world considered to be of outstanding universal value to humanity. Hadrian's Wall is one of these sites, inscribed in the World Heritage List in 1987, and now part of the Frontiers of the Roman Empire World Heritage property.

The aim of the World Heritage Convention is not just to preserve important sites, but also to encourage countries to work harmoniously together to protect the joint heritage of humankind and to learn from each other. The Frontiers of the Roman Empire project is an excellent example of this as archaeologists and cultural resource managers from a dozen countries in Europe, together with UNESCO, are pursuing the joint aim of creating and managing a multi-country World Heritage site.

The Frontiers of the Roman Empire is not simply a linear World Heritage site. Roman armies advanced well beyond the permanent frontiers and left their mark in the form of military installations. In the hinterland of the frontiers lie other forts marking stages in advance or retreat - or supporting the front-line troops through 'defence-in-depth'. The permanent frontiers therefore sit within a broader landscape. This book is primarily a guide to part of that landscape. It is also a celebration of the life of the Roman emperor who, more than any other, created the frontiers, forts, fortlets and towers which form the basis of the World Heritage site and which still offer a challenging research puzzle for today's archaeologists and explorers.

I am convinced that this book provides an in-depth analysis and new insights into a fascinating and complex serial transnational World Heritage site.

Mechtild Rössler

Director of the UNESCO World Heritage Centre in Paris.

UNESCO

United Nations
Educational, Scientific and
Cultural Organization

Frontiers of the
Roman Empire
inscribed on the World
Heritage List in 2005

HADRIAN'S HIGH WAY

A Journey Through Time

The World's first
PEACE TRAIL

A Journey Through Time

This guide has been prepared to coincide with the momentous 1,900th anniversary of Hadrian's accession as Emperor, on 11th August 2017.

When Hadrian inherited the empire, Britannia was in a sorry state. His predecessor Trajan, having withdrawn legions to wage war in Dacia and Mesopotamia, had allowed the British tribes, such as the local Brigantes, almost free rein. Hadrian subsequently struck a coin in AD 119, following an unspecified battle, that shows the subjugation of the Britons. Further battles followed, leading to the ultimate statement of his control - the building of the Wall, reflecting both Hadrian's personal passion for architecture and respect for the military life. Throughout his reign he sought to instil order and unity of purpose and to secure the Empire's bounds. If you lived south of the Wall you were obliged to abide by the Roman rulebook.

2017 also marks the 30th anniversary of the original designation (1987) by UNESCO of Hadrian's Wall as a World Heritage Site.

With good reason Hadrian is often cited as the 'Peacemaker', and this marries with the original thinking behind such a designation, which endeavours to elevate the cultural and natural landscape of the world for greater mutual understanding and peace. Indeed, UNESCO's first statute states: "That since wars begin in the minds of men, it is in the minds of men that the defences of peace must be constructed". Hence I was thrilled when Mechtild Rössler offered her wholehearted support for this guide by writing a foreword. In keeping with the founding principles of UNESCO I have ascribed Hadrian's High Way a PEACE TRAIL, my motivation being to open readers' minds to reflect on their own personal understanding of the word 'peace' experienced when walking in the natural environment, looking at communities and heritage first hand. From this, they may then consider the underlying values of UNESCO, wherein peace conveys a far deeper global meaning for humanity. This route, which covers the Lake District National Park, the North Pennines AONB Global Geopark and Hadrian's Wall, together with the Northumberland National Park, celebrates the unity of conservation, cultural heritage and, most of all, people.

A walk of a thousand miles - or 102 miles in this case - starts with the first step. Your first step along Hadrian's High Way is off the train and onto the platform at Ravenglass Station on the Cumbrian Coast Line. Your initial thought may be to walk onto the tidal shore at the end of Ravenglass Main Street and survey the meeting of the waters. Three rivers converge here and are held in check by two great sand bars forming a sheltered haven, a natural harbour that in all probability has been used from time immemorial. However, we know that it was a vital haven for the Romans and, when Hadrian's great frontier was constructed, this was its westernmost point.

This is the start of Hadrian's fantastic frontier. All the way up the Cumbrian coast mileforts and major forts were installed, to which considerable civil settlements (vici, sing. vicus) were attached - a defence against the aggressive behaviour of the Selgovae tribe, in what we now call Dumfries and Galloway.

From the great estuary of the Eden, the Solway Firth, an outrageous stone wall was built, although under Hadrian the first 32 miles running east was a turf bank, built because of the lack of local mortar and sandstone. Some one hundred years on - despite all the logistical challenges - a stone curtain wall was completed from Bowness-on-Solway, though the tidal inundations on Burgh Marshes made it impossible to build a continuous stone water-tight wall.

Hadrian's High Way takes a dynamic new look at that frontier, but not by trekking up the Cumbrian coast, which has been transformed over the succeeding 1,900 years. Instead our journey embraces the majestic hinterland inland from the coast and through which the Roman garrisons marched, supporting tight order on their jurisdiction for 300 years.

Hadrian sought to convey the irresistible power of Roman rule. He built audacious forts, such as Hard Knott, and throughout the journey we will see that once there stood many other great stations of command. We get a very real sense of the challenges the Romans faced in supplying and running the northern limit of their great empire. We see the landscape much as they may have viewed it in practical terms. They knew how to move intelligently through a wild land, up dales and over passes. Their routes, meticulously surveyed with grids on angles and slope pitches, kept to the most economical lines. They also took early advantage of native routes. It was upon one such that they even created a myth that has lasted to the present day. While they may have adapted the age-old High Street ridge for imperial effect, they did not use it for regular movement. Indeed, why would they expend such effort when they could, as we do today, keep to the valleys? After all, they were the conquering force, although it must be acknowledged that an excavation in 2006, where Scot Rake meets the skyline ridge, revealed a typical substrate-inverted Roman agger.

So they gifted us a journey that is as relevant today as in Roman times. There is no better way to view fell country than to follow the Roman road east, from the port at Ravenglass, their maritime link with the empire. Passing through the wild mountains, we ultimately trace the actual frontier along the Great Whin Sill, where the Wall sits proud upon a striking escarpment within Northumberland National Park. This is a real journey of discovery, linking ten forts, each in turn vital connections underpinning life on the Wall. It stretches for just over 100 miles, through a constantly changing, thoroughly absorbing and spellbindingly beautiful landscape - in sun, wind or rain - culminating in a euphoric, personal triumph as you stride beside the actual Roman Wall.

The journey begins impressively, visiting the remarkably tall Walls Castle, the bath-house remains attached to the fort of Glannoventa. Advancing up the Esk, we climb by Hard Knott Roman fort and slip over the awesome pass into the Duddon. Forging on now over Wrynose Pass into Little Langdale, we head for Skelwith Bridge, climbing over the shoulder of Todd Crag to enter Ambleside, where the third fort is found.

This is an important point of decision for walkers. The regular Roman roads headed north via Dunmail Raise, east via Kirkstone Pass and south alongside Windermere, heading for Kendal and their fort at Watercrook. They also adapted the pre-existing native route via Troutbeck, climbing onto High Street, which was a considerable energy-sapping march, then as now. This has been adopted as the primary route of Hadrian's High Way, just as much to emphasise the ancient use of this ridge as to stress its dubious Roman connections.

High Street is a big day, whatever the size of your boots, so a more manageable alternative is described over Scandale Pass and Boredale Hause, bringing Patterdale and Martindale into the equation. The principal route follows a lane across the slopes of Wansfell Pike to the delightful village of Troutbeck, before taking to Scot Rake to reach the highest point on the route on High Street, with no doubting how this mountain gained its name.

The ridge north ultimately comes down upon The Cockpit stone circle and meets up with the alternative route, veering off the strict line of the Roman road shown on Ordnance Survey maps to sustain the quality of the walking in visiting Lowther Park and Clifton, before venturing on by Brougham Hall and Eamont

Bridge. This is also the half-way point and end of Part One, with a connection to Penrith for the station.

Part Two continues the journey by Brougham Castle, where we find the fourth fort, Brocavum, and enjoys the glorious splendour of the Eden valley to Kirkby Thore, site of the fifth fort, Bravoniacum. Heading on by Milburn and Kirkland, the route takes on a further mountain leg, and this time there is no doubting its Roman authenticity, following the Maiden Way over the Pennine watershed of Melmerby Fell to reach Alston. During the short grouse-shooting period, or after very heavy rain, a variant route is recommended, crossing the ridge to Garrigill and so down the South Tyne with the Pennine Way, visiting the sixth fort of Epiacum and then the seventh fort, Magna at Carvoran, where the Vindolanda Trust has its Roman Army Museum. The final leg follows the Whin Sill scarp, soaking up Hadrian's Wall ultimate exhibition with two further forts, Aesica (Great Chesters) and Vercovicum (Housesteads), before finally switching south via Vindolanda to end at Bardon Mill station on the Tyne Valley Line.

How much time you devote to walking the route is entirely up to you. Many walkers have the stamina and experience to undertake the whole 100-mile trek in 9 or 10 days. Far better, though, to break it up into two week-long walking holidays. But you can also take it in neat, short bite-sized portions.

Remember, too, that you don't have to walk all the high ground to participate in the adventure. Notably the highest stretch, along the great skyline of the High Street range, can be honourably side-stepped by crossing the passes by Patterdale and Martindale. The escapism, joys and beauties just roll and roll as you amble, ramble and unscramble the riches of our rural heritage along the corridor of Hadrian's High Way.

Ravenglass - the amazing journey begins

The colourful little village of Ravenglass is deservedly embraced within the Lake District National Park, its one street opening onto the sheltered tidal shore where the rivers Esk, Mite and Irt mingle with the saltwater of the Irish Sea. It's a fishing village, yet belongs to Eskdale, with maritime and mountain a lovely combination, enhanced by the connection provided by 'La'al Ratty', the miniature railway.

1   From the Cumbrian Coast Line station, descend the approach to Main Street with the ship mosaic motif ahead, a striking reminder of Ravenglass's long tradition as a maritime haven and a place of fishing and adventure. Your personal adventure is underway (and you might like to know that the Ravenglass & Eskdale Railway station has a great café).

2   Turn left and wander to The Pennington (hotel and restaurant-bar). You have two options to reach the Walls Castle drive. Turn promptly left, following an alley to the edge of the village car park, advancing to cross a footbridge over the Cumbrian Coast Line - a fine vantage from which to see the branch line terminus of

ROUTE MAP 1

1 Km   1 Mile

← NORTH →

King George IV

Forge Bridge

Eskdale Green

7

Muncaster Head

Roman tile kilns
(low mounds)

Irton Road

River Mite

Silver
Knott

River Esk

Ross's
Camp

High Eskholme

Roman road?

Ravenglass &
Eskdale Railway

La'al Ratty

Muncaster Fell
Hooker Crag   231m 758ft △

Esk Trail

6

Muncaster Tarn

Muncaster Castle

5

Glannoventa
Bath House

A595

8

1

RAVENGLASS

2

3

4

Cumbrian
Coast Railway

Irish Sea

La'al Ratty, the miniature railway. This one-time iron-ore line derives its name from its rattling carriages. The path leads onto the start of the drive, beside the caravan park - turn right and watch for the Esk Trail waymarking, guiding you onto the adjacent tree-weaving pathway leading to the Roman bath-house ruins.

At low tide perhaps the more appealing route continues along the village street, fronted by its attractive mingle of prettily painted cottages. At the far end a metal gate forms an ocean barrier, only closed when exceptional tides are pending. Go through and bear left along the sandy shoreline, seeking the footpath that leads back left to an underpass of the railway, bringing you neatly onto the Walls Castle drive.

Walls Castle is remarkable, with sandstone walls standing some twelve feet high and holding several rooms. That it has survived must point to the structure

Glannoventa bath-house; Ravenglass

finding a later purpose, as otherwise the stones would have long since been 'borrowed'. The bath-house stood outside the fort of Glannoventa, the low banks and rush -filled ditches of which are faintly visible over the field-gate to the right of the track. On the far side spot a small tapered pillar of unknown origin. Behind the bath-house lay the extensive civil settlement (vicus). Some of the excavated finds are on display at The Pennington in the village. The interpretative panels are well worth reading and give a strong clue to what the fort and settlement were like 1,900 years ago. The Roman road that is the inspiration for this walk has not been categorically determined, but the lie of the land suggests it went up by Decoy Drive, our next objective.

3 From the seat, the footway runs on beside the tarmac drive, bearing left along the track, with an Esk Trail fingerpost (blue board 'Knott View' on the right and 'Newtown House', left). Take the next track left; purple sign, 'Muncaster' Esk Trail fingerpost. Follow the enchanting track up the wooded dingle, passing a pond and by open gates, coming along a fenced lane flanked by pasture to enter woodland. Ignore the footpath signed left with the track. Go straight on, guided by the Esk Trail fingerpost, to reach the public entrance and rotunda pavilion to Muncaster Castle. Rhododendrons are profuse and, in early summer, a glorious embellishment. You may care to acquire a ticket and spend an hour or two perusing the wonderful wooded gardens and the castle itself.

Otherwise, bear left to exit the stone gateway, very cautiously crossing the busy road; traffic comes upon you very quickly, so not only look but listen intently before you cross. Either follow the main road (the footway is briefly lost as it passes the old primary school) or, better, enter the large car park, advancing as per the Esk Trail fingerpost via the gate and open track. Where the track forks, veer right, away from the farm, rising easily to a gate at the road bend; now turn left up Fell Lane.

4 As an interesting variation you may wish to pass through Muncaster Castle grounds (passing the Owl Centre cafe) and this can simply be achieved in a loop back to the foot of Fell Lane as indicated on the map. Pass on from the Esk Trail indicated track, seeking a

Muncaster Castle

hand-gate into woodland on the left, adjacent to Newtown House. The path leads up to a fence-stile into pasture. Angle half-left up the rushy sheep pasture to a kissing-gate in the high park wall. The pathway leads down through the woodland famous for its exotic mix of trees and rhododendrons to cross the lawns as indicated by waymarking, with the impressive Muncaster Castle over to the right.

The Castle would appear to be set upon a Roman watch tower site, which explains the 'caster' element in the name. Staggeringly it has been in the Pennington family since 1208. The oldest parts of the present castle are the great hall and peel tower which are C14th, gloriously remodelled in the 1860s. It well deserves a full day's visit and has its own naughty ghost, that of Tom Skelton. Pass up the lane by the estate office, by the café and the entrance to the hugely popular Hawk and Owl Centre which features exciting live displays. St. Michael's church merits a visit, this includes Pre-Raphaelite stained glass and, like the Castle, shows the influence of Victorian architect Anthony Salvin. After the parish church, meet the road and turn left with the roadside footway.

5 Ascending within the metalled Fell Lane, there is a possibility that you are now following in Roman footsteps. Backward glances remind you of the maritime situation for one last time, with the Isle of Man a striking feature on the western horizon, rising to the high point of Snaefell. As the track descends, take a little glance left to see Muncaster Tarn, a peaceful sheet of water surrounded by trees, the near area spread with lovely lilies. As the track continues, watch for the three-way fingerpost.

6 You have two route options: the damp open ridge of **Muncaster Fell** or the firm, dry **Esk Trail**.

The primary route turns sharp right, accompanying the **Esk Trail**. The path swings left and, after a gate, heads smartly downhill beside tall trees, with a newly felled plantation up the slope to the left. En route, spot Chapel's Tower behind a private dwelling. The three-storey octagonal spired tower is a monument to Henry VI, probably built in the 18th century. It is said to mark the place where shepherds found Henry VI wandering the fells after the battle of Towton in 1461. Tradition has it that Henry VI arrived at nearby Irton Hall and sought shelter. Being refused by the owner, a Yorkist, King Henry spent the night under the great oak in front of the house, which still stands and is hence called 'The King's Oak'. The next day Henry fled over the fell to Muncaster where Sir John Pennington gave the king food and shelter for as long as he requested it. In gratitude, Henry gave Sir John a glass drinking bowl and said it was given to the family with a prayer that they might prosper for as long as the glass remained unbroken. The glass – known as 'The Luck of Muncaster' - remains unbroken to this day and the family has prospered.

Reaching a shed, currently painted green, step onto the tarmac drive, then pass a mini-Ashness Bridge garden feature overlooking a shy golf course, then passing three dwellings at High Eskholme. The drive becomes a track after passing a car parking area, now with lovely dale-bottom views across the Esk valley pastures. Passing felled areas, most notable to the right on the peaty expanse of Parkhouse Moss, the track is beautifully lined with native woodland with the odd rhododendron. You need to keep a keen eye out for a small green cast-iron board to the right, indicating the site of Roman tile kilns, identified as a low mound. After a galvanised gate, pass on unhindered by Muncaster Head Farm, where the ridge route connects.

Muncaster Fell Ridge Route The track rises easily on to a double gate, shrouded with rhododendron bushes. Quickly opening onto the fell, the path leads purposefully on beside the forest fence. You may be tempted to visit the summit of Muncaster Fell, where the stone-built Ordnance Survey pillar on Hooker Crag commands a fabulous viewpoint at 231m (758ft), overlooking to the east a large marshy bowl of cotton grass that is the origin of the summit-name, hooker or 'hollow carr'.

The modest height belies the wide panoramic view above the plain north to Sellafield, St. Bees Head and the Roman coastal frontier, but more impressively east and south to the great Lakeland mountains, with Scafell and company the most striking to the north-east. However, there is an old ridge path which weaves and undulates gently through the marshy moor grass to the south of Hooker Crag, leading by Ross's Camp (a stone table, inscribed 1883). The path bears down left - keep left to skirt a notably damp hollow, joining the popular ridge path from Hooker Crag that leads to a gateway at a wall corner. The footpath descends, although the wet ground close to the wall ensures that the walker disregards the green-dashed line indicated on Ordnance Survey maps.

The popular line of desire drifts right from the wall and comes into a hollow, where it connects with a striking green way set on a sharply rising shelf with a retaining wall. It's impossible to judge how old this is, as the cutting at the top is comparatively modern yet surely set upon an ancient course. Lined by ancient standing stone markers, the 'road' leads, in effect, down the south side of Silver Knott to reach a kissing-gate with an old sheepfold in the wet corner. The path leads on, brushing gorse in the Rabbit How enclosure, to reach the open track. Turn right via gates to reach Muncaster Head Farm - heed the 'beware of bulls' notice if you have a dog. There is an alternative bridleway leading direct to Eskdale Green station as a practical opt-out.

Coming onto the track in front of the farmhouse, turn left with the Esk Trail, which leads over a fine stone bridge spanning the River Esk to reach the road at Forge House Farm. Turn left to Forge Bridge, a popular spot to paddle and play in the bouldery beck. Beyond the bridge, the road leads to Eskdale Green, with the King George IV pub at the junction being a dog-friendly establishment with a great welcome.

7 The High Way, however, does not cross the bridge. Instead it follows the inviting track marked with a fingerpost for the Esk Trail to 'Stanley Ghyll and Dalegarth Station'. The track accompanies the clear waters of the Esk upstream, coming to a gate/cattle grid after which the track leads through an open meadow. Head on by a gate, now within a fenced lane passing a suspension footbridge. After the next gate enter woodland and pass the ruins of the old Milkingstead Farm, with its cobbled yard underfoot. A sinuous path leads through birch woodland and over a bedrock rise to go through a gate. In the next wooded section see if you can spot a small smoot hole, built into the base of the adjacent wall for ensnaring rabbits. The woodland is something of an arboretum with many soaring trees.

After another gate you will soon see the five conical Westmorland-style chimneys of Dalegarth Hall, down the field to the left, which is the capital house of the valley and which has been standing on this site since 1345. To the right, you get a first real glimpse of Scafell through the trees. Head on by further gates, ignoring the crossing track from Dalegarth Station to the falls, guided by the sign for Doctor's Bridge. Descend a pasture to enter a mature conifer woodland; at a gate, the path crosses a wooden footbridge spanning Birker Beck. Another gate leads out of the wood, with a first sight of Harter Fell ahead.

8 Immediately, the route takes the right-hand fork (the path straight ahead leads to the stepping stones to St

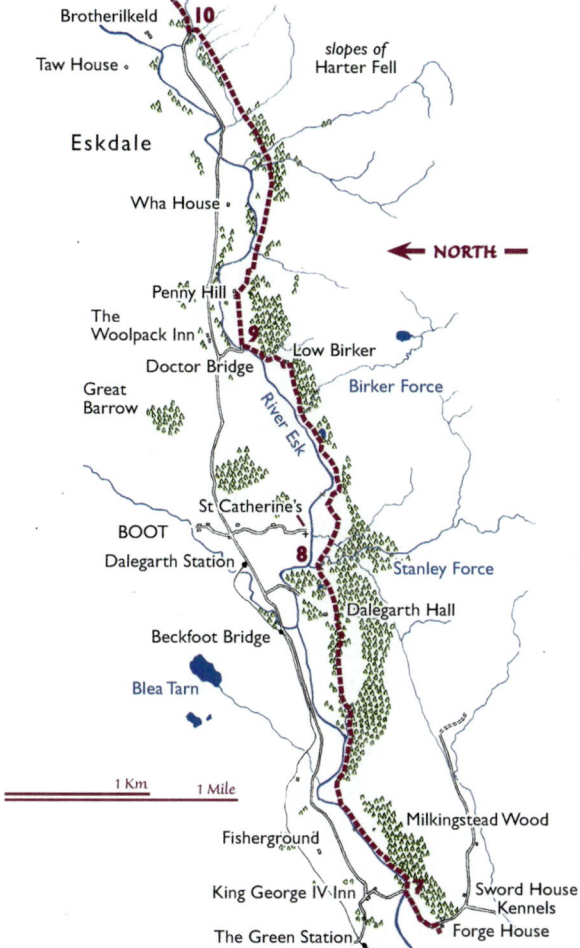

ROUTE MAP 2

HARD KNOTT
Roman fort

Brotherilkeld

Taw House

slopes of
Harter Fell

Eskdale

Wha House

← NORTH —

Penny Hill

The
Woolpack Inn

9

Low Birker

Doctor Bridge

Great
Barrow

Birker Force

River Esk

St Catherine's

BOOT

8

Dalegarth Station

Stanley Force

Dalegarth Hall

Beckfoot Bridge

Blea Tarn

1 Km   1 Mile

Milkingstead Wood

Fisherground

King George IV Inn

Sword House
Kennels

The Green Station

Forge House

17

Catherine's church and the little village of Boot). The path slips through a ford and takes a left-hand bend around a wall corner. Keep forward, as directed by a bridleway (blue waymark) post at a fork in the path; this leads to a gate/stile. Turn right, signed 'Low Birker', advancing via a gate into more open country and soon passing a lily-filled tarn screened by an unnecessary line of conifers. Ahead, you'll see Scafell and the flat-top fell of Crinkle Crags, known from this angle appropriately as Long Top.

There's yet another gate and promptly a footbridge over Low Birker Gill - head on with a wall close to your right, with a view left to Little and Great Barrow. Entering a walled lane section, make a point of switching down by Low Birker Farm, its agricultural identity long lost. The drive leads down via a cattle-grid/gate to Doctor's Bridge, from where the road can be joined to visit The Woolpack Inn, an ever-popular destination.

9 The High Way turns right along the access lane to Penny Hill Farm (National Trust). Straight as a die, the lane strongly suggests it overlays the Roman road - reminiscent of Fell Lane climbing onto Muncaster Fell. Keep on through the cobbled farmyard. The white-washed farmhouse is in splendid order, as is the garden, even though this is a working farm (formerly called Pyot's Nest, with the screech of magpies occasionally heard in the vicinity). The ensuing walled lane opens at a gate into pasture.

The track leads invitingly on, still in all probability the Roman road. The next gate offers a fine view of Harter Fell, with a specimen Scots pine for photographic composition. The track leads on via a small ford to a gate, then heads forward in pasture with a green way, although the Roman route probably drifted lower below the wall and screening trees. From the next gate the track hugs the left-hand wall to a gate/stile into woodland, shading a gill which is forded.

Arriving at a three-way footpath sign keep forward as following the sign to 'Jubilee Bridge'. The path crosses a plank footbridge and some stony ground to slip through a gate and follow a wall with open views left towards Bowfell and Crinkle Crags. Pass through a kissing-gate, step over a small gill and traverse the bracken slope on a clear path. After the next kissing-gate, the path leads through an area planted with young deciduous trees (in plastic sheaths). After a small ford, the path rises by a fence corner to merge with a bridle-path from Dunnerdale. Go through the two gates to cross the diminutive Jubilee Bridge (a stone footbridge) to join the road beside the cattle-grid.

10 Ascend the road above the lay-by - the sign suggests 'severe bends' for drivers, though not the kind experienced by divers rising hastily from aquatic depths! If the bracken is low you may veer left onto the fell as the left-hand wall breaks left. Otherwise, continue with the road until a suitable breach path in the bracken suggests a less entangled route direct to the western wall of the Roman fort.

The Scafell massif from the north gate of Hard Knott Roman fort

All the stone below the thin slate course is original Roman construction, treated to prevent collapse. Above this, the wall has been reconstructed from fallen Roman facing stones to a height of not more than 6'6" which was the maximum height of the original work found in position. Inside the fort the bare outline walls of numerous internal buildings can be seen, as well as the corner turrets. It is a wild setting, little different from the landscape known to the 2nd-century AD Dalmatian garrison (modern-day Croatia). It is a grand place to explore. Trace the bounding walls and even visit the bath-house, down the slope a little way to the south-east. No less impressive are the backing fells at the head of Eskdale, the mighty Scafells.

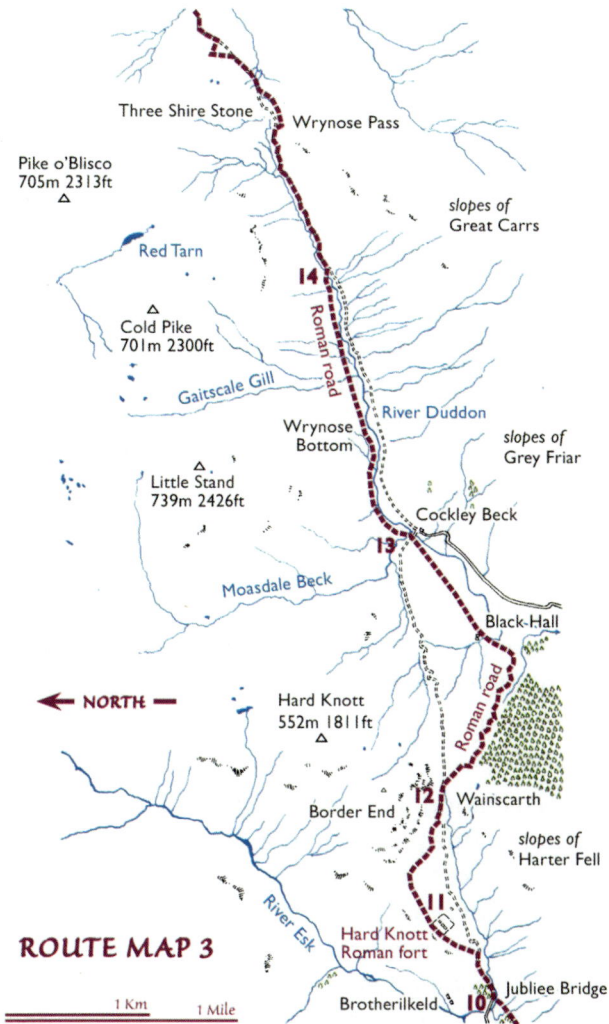

Three Shire Stone   Wrynose Pass

Pike o'Blisco
705m 2313ft

slopes of
Great Carrs

Red Tarn

14

Roman road

Cold Pike
701m 2300ft

Gaitscale Gill

River Duddon

Wrynose
Bottom

slopes of
Grey Friar

Little Stand
739m 2426ft

Cockley Beck

13

Moasdale Beck

Black-Hall

← NORTH →

Hard Knott
552m 1811ft

Roman road

12   Wainscarth

Border End

slopes of
Harter Fell

11

ROUTE MAP 3

River Esk

Hard Knott
Roman fort

Jubliee Bridge

Brotherilkeld   **10**

1 Km   1 Mile

21

11 Moving on, venture across the Roman parade ground, a great expanse of flat pasture devoid of stone. The Romans swept it clear and heaped the stones into a rostrum on the north-west side, comprising 5,000 cubic metres of rock that would have been surmounted with a shrine. The Roman road is thought not to have traversed the parade ground, though that is where the footpath traipses and naturally draws under Border End, reconnecting with the Roman way just before an obvious notch leading onto the modern road at a hairpin. Note the drop down, showing the modern road engineers cut into the Roman way. Turn to climb with the road almost to the summit of the pass. This was known in former times as Wainscarth - the 'wagon pass' - indicative of its continued use into medieval times as a trade route to the coast.

12 Short of the summit, watch for the public bridleway signpost indicating the point of departure from the modern tarmac road. A clear track, with evidence of Roman rubble cobbling, takes a southern turn. This way crosses the line of a low broken wall and draws towards a fence, before veering to the left.

It is a fascinating journey down to Black Hall Farm. Tantalising suggestions of the route the Roman road might have taken keep one guessing, and frequently one has considerable confidence that one is dead on it, with much mossiness taken in one's stride. Cross a ladder-stile beside a fenced sheep-creep en route down, and note the bog myrtle soon after. Lower down it becomes more certain and it ultimately curves left, as countless shepherds have been inclined to follow suit. The open Roman way draws down to run above the intake wall. Go through the right-hand of two field-gates (waymarked) in the corner. Turn left, advancing toward Black Hall (National Trust farm/one-time youth hostel). The footpath has been provided with a by-pass via stile/hand-gates, though there is little hazard in going through the farmyard itself, directly onto the farm access track, which is most definitely plumb upon the Roman road. The open track gives a wonderful feeling of marching in Roman footsteps. After a gate the track emerges onto the road close by Cockley Beck Bridge.

13 The Roman way persists as a ford over Mosedale Beck. A footpath way follows suit, but via a slate plank footbridge set into the adjacent wall, accessed from a wall-stile. The wet ground can be churned up, since the rough dale-bottom pasture is presently the home to a herd of Belted Galloway cattle. Follow on beside the River Duddon fence, frequently being conscious that for all the wash-out over the centuries there is still some evidence of the ancient agger. A field-gate with stile is encountered where a wall merges from the left - continue with much marshiness and uncertainty of being on any form of a road. While you may be tempted left, the actual way heads across the mosses to emerge as a very plausible causeway with stone agger.

Next, go through a wide hand-gate beside the river, set into a newly rebuilt wall, and then cross the stile over to the left in the fenced enclosure. Possibly the worst marsh intervenes, so keep left to avoid this. Ford the stony Gaitscale Gill, now in open access land. Walk along the slope, avoiding the dale bottom marsh. Frequently the cattle linger at the furthest meadow. Where the ground is driest and as the riverside fence is replaced by a wall, find a stile and skip over the infant River Duddon to step onto the modern road.

14 The sinuous ribbon of tarmac is your guide to the top of the pass. The actual Roman road crossed to the

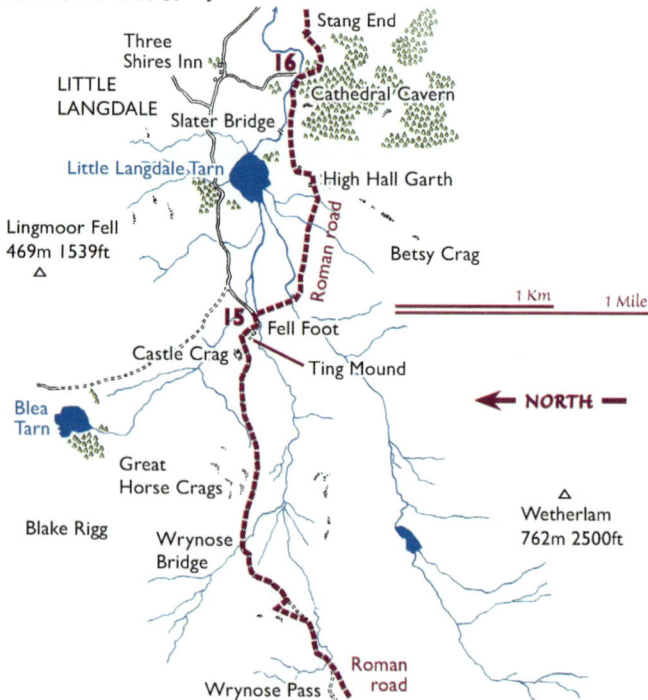

ROUTE MAP 4

Stang End

Three Shires Inn

16

LITTLE LANGDALE

Cathedral Cavern

Slater Bridge

Little Langdale Tarn

High Hall Garth

Roman road

Lingmoor Fell 469m 1539ft △

Betsy Crag

1 Km   1 Mile

15 Fell Foot

Castle Crag

Ting Mound

Blea Tarn

← NORTH →

Great Horse Crags

△ Wetherlam 762m 2500ft

Blake Rigg

Wrynose Bridge

Wrynose Pass

Roman road

right of the modern road and then beyond the Three Shires Stone striking across to the north side amongst the rock and bracken. It is hard to spot with certainty, apart from an obvious zig-zag track that suggests an ancient course. The Roman road actually swept well above Wrynose Bridge and, where the fellside steepens, ran down quite a way up from the modern road, though centuries of landslipping has all but wiped it away.

Follow the road down, coming by Castle Crag, descriptive of the rock rather than any former bastion. You may go through the kissing-gate in the wall on the right to inspect the Ting Mound, a gathering place in Viking times. Otherwise keep with the road, swinging right to pass in front of Fell Foot farmhouse and, after the left-hand bend, seek the public way signed 'Tilberthwaite', posted right.

15 It has been judged that the Roman road deviates from the line of the modern road beyond Fell Foot, in suit with the track leading to the south of Little Langdale Tarn, sustaining an eastward course on the south side of the valley. It's a great boon as this line provides the best walking. So, buoyed with the knowledge that you are still in tune with the ancient way, slip through the generous kissing-gate and follow the track via a gate at Bridge End, a lovely traditional farmhouse with integral byre.

The track advances as an open stony way on a gentle rise and passes the joining track from Greenburn. Keep left at the Tilberthwaite fork - where you can see water erosion has denuded the track to bedrock. Go through

Slater Bridge

the gate and follow the walled lane by High Hall Garth, now beneath a great pile of slate spoil, coming down to the Yorkshire Ramblers' Club hut at Low Hall Garth. Beyond, you may well be tempted to visit Slater Bridge, arguably the most exquisite stone arched footbridge in England. It's accessed from a kissing-gate and reached across a short meadow – backtrack to continue.

The lane next goes through a gate and shortly after there is another lure to the right at a gate; an inclined track leading to Cathedral Cavern (old slate quarry), again a fabulous sight to behold and safe to enter with due caution. The main track passes a footbridge and

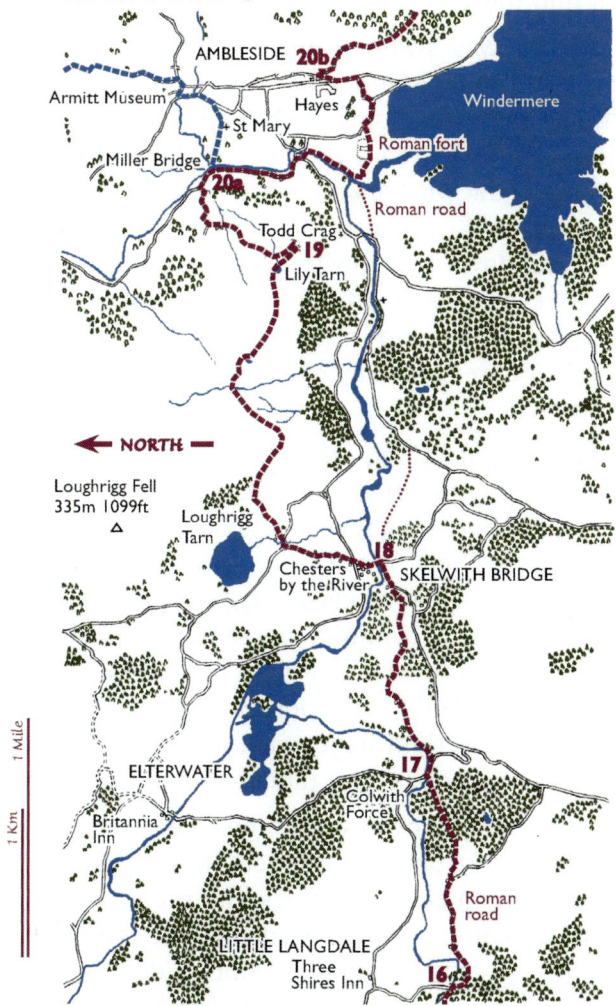

ROUTE MAP 5

AMBLESIDE **20b**

Armitt Museum

Hayes

Windermere

St Mary

Roman fort

Miller Bridge

20a

Roman road

Todd Crag

19

Lily Tarn

← NORTH →

Loughrigg Fell
335m 1099ft
△

Loughrigg
Tarn

18

Chesters
by the River

SKELWITH BRIDGE

1 Mile

1 Km

ELTERWATER

17

Colwith
Force

Britannia
Inn

Roman
road

LITTLE LANGDALE
Three
Shires Inn

16

27

deep ford - access to Little Langdale hamlet - where you'll find the Three Shires Inn.

16 The roadway swings right and advances by a cattle grid up through Stang End to High Park, where the multi-use footway is signed through the yard. Head on through the facing gate with the newly made path via a field-gate, now with a wall left entering woodland at a gate. Keep to the right-hand wallside path (the left-hand path leads down by Colwith Force waterfall should you wish to see it, best after recent rain obviously). The main way comes down to a fork; go left, weaving through the trees to duly exit the wood via a hand-gate and steps.

17 Turn right along the road, soon finding the continuing way left at a wall-stile. The made path winds across the short meadow to a stile and embarks on a flight of steps to a fence-stile. Traverse the field on a clear path to a metal kissing-gate and head on by a hand-gate into a confined passage, exiting at a wall squeeze-stile followed by a stile in a wall to enter the yard of Elterwater Park. Spot early the slate alphabet sample on the right-hand wall, en route conversing, perhaps, with the resident tame hens!

Exit at a gate: following the lane, the open track slips through a short passage by metal kissing-gates at Park House. Head on along the track and then an open made path to a hand-gate into woodland. At the next three-way sign go right, signed 'Ambleside', via a gate, exiting the woodland along a made path opening onto the Coniston road. Go left, watchful of traffic, and swing left to cross Skelwith Bridge. The Chesters by the River café suggests a Roman fort, though the name derives from a pet dog of the same name!

18 Follow the main road verge to the junction with the Langdale road and cross over by the bus shelter to ascend the minor road, climbing by Neaum Brow and Crag. Bear right at the T-junction and then left at Tarn Foot, advancing to a gate into a walled lane - a slate sign reads 'To Ambleside'. With a tall wall on the right the path bends right to a further gate; keep company with the wall below the bracken-clad fellside. The popular path advances onto the open fell, restored by substrate inversion to cope with the heavy pedestrian traffic. You can continue straight on, descending through the old Ambleside golf course, though far better is to visit the top of Todd Crag with its superb

Looking down on the head of Windermere and Ambleside Roman fort from below Todd Crag

view of the Roman fort, close to the head of Windermere.

At the high point, find a path breaking right through the bracken. This crosses a crest and bears right and left to a kissing-gate then, with a wall on the right, opens again to pass Lily Tarn, with its bog bean and solitary birch. The rocky knott of Todd Crag (a reference to foxes) marks the culmination of the ridge and a place to pause and soak up the amazing view south down Windermere. See the confluence of the rivers Brathay and Rothay as they mingle to flow into the great lake and, to the left, the fenced enclosure on the meadow of Ambleside Roman fort, soon to be visited en route.

19 Cut back and veer right through the bracken to find your way down to a kissing-gate. The next bracken-filled enclosure has young trees in individual fences to keep deer out. The oft-eroded path descends quite steeply, latterly by steps, to a footbridge and then along a lateral path at the base of a wood to steps leading down onto the tarmac road (the continuation of the earlier route through the old golf course). The road winds down, quite steeply latterly, to meet the Under Loughrigg Road.

Go right, via the cattle-grid, reaching Miller Bridge footbridge, where you have two serious route options to consider: (A) the imperious high-road used from antiquity, with the great traverse of the High Street range, or (B) the alternative fell trek that breaks the journey in two at Patterdale, crossing Scandale Pass and Boredale Hause.

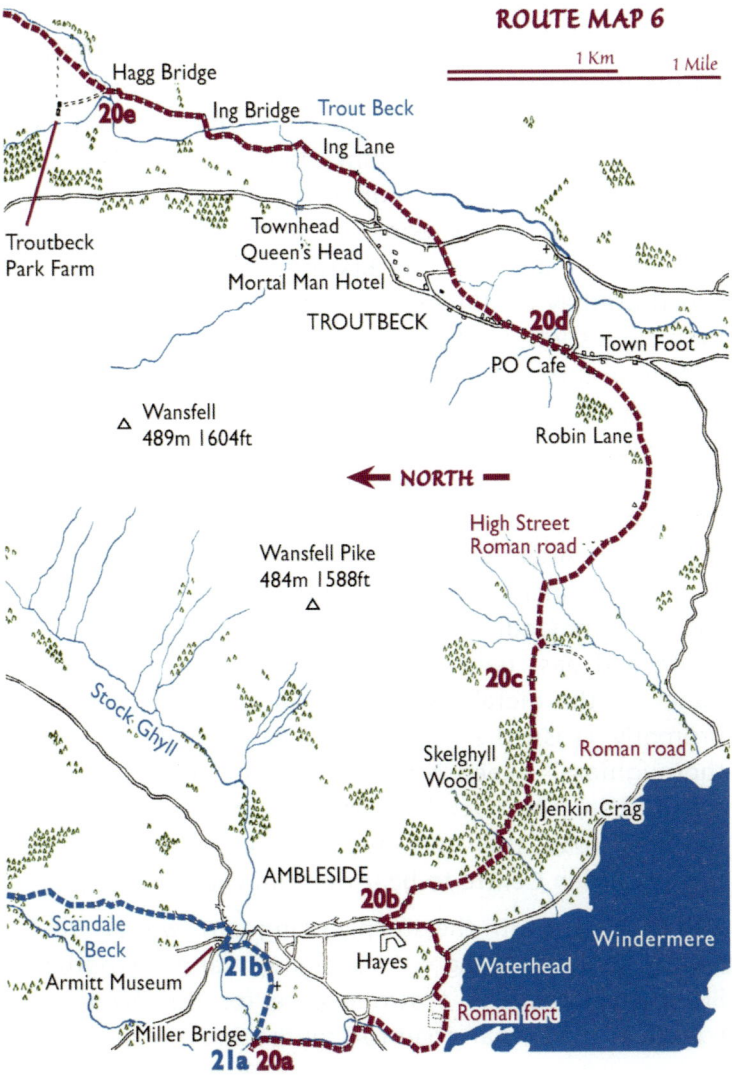

ROUTE MAP 6

1 Km   1 Mile

Hagg Bridge

20e

Ing Bridge   Trout Beck

Ing Lane

Troutbeck
Park Farm

Townhead
Queen's Head
Mortal Man Hotel

TROUTBECK   **20d**

Town Foot

PO Cafe

△ Wansfell
  489m 1604ft

Robin Lane

← NORTH →

High Street
Roman road

Wansfell Pike
484m 1588ft
△

20c

Stock Ghyll

Skelghyll
Wood   Roman road

Jenkin Crag

AMBLESIDE   **20b**

Scandale
Beck

Armitt Museum   Hayes   Windermere

21b   Waterhead

Miller Bridge   Roman fort

21a 20a

31

Ambleside to The Cockpit via High Street

20a The primary route follows the Under Loughrigg Road to the junction with the Langdale road (A593). Cautiously cross the road and follow the footpath right to cross the arched footbridge over the River Rothay. From the hand-gate, turn immediately right through the field-gate. At times of high water this route may be submerged or overly damp at least! Follow the river downstream and after two kissing-gates you'll pass the broad Brathay confluence – a natural bathing pool! The path curves left, via two further kissing-gates and duck-boarding, through Birdhouse Meadow to enter the large field with the Wonder of Windermere panel, containing the fenced portions of the Roman fort. Maps continue to annotate this as Galava, though this is probably a mis-appropriation. Take the opportunity to look within the fenced areas where key central buildings are well evidenced, including the headquarters (with strong room), commanding officer's house, granaries and the south and east gates. Exit from the main information panel via the metal kissing-gate into Borrans Park and promptly cross the road by the bollards (it's a busy thoroughfare) - keep right. Coming by Wateredge Inn, turn left into Maciver Lane and follow this through to the main road, then turn left with the footway passing Hayes Garden Centre to bear right up Old Lake Road.

20b Bear right with the steeply rising narrow road (rusty sign) 'Jenkins Crag – Skelghyll and Troutbeck Bridleway'. There is a strong case for this being the course of the Roman road to Troutbeck. Look back over your shoulder to see Todd Crag overtopping the Mountain Rescue building and soon look down on the great glassy amphitheatre of Hayes Garden Centre. Keep course with directions for Skelghyll Woods at each fork in the way, to come by the National Trust sign heralding entry into the woods themselves. Keeping to the bridleway (cycle logo on waymarks) you'll come up a stony bedrock trail swinging right over a bridge and, soon after levelling, you may opt to visit the Jenkin Crag viewpoint on a spur. Otherwise, keep with the gently rising track to level, passing the tell-tale sandstone gateposts and metal hand-gates that indicate precisely where the Thirlmere Aqueduct strikes through, bound for Manchester! Shortly, a gate brings the path out of the wood on a largely level track, leading via gates through the environs of High Skelghyll Farm.

20c Follow on down the road and at the three-way sign keep with the bridleway signed 'Troutbeck', going by the fold and filled-in grid over the bridge to a succession of hand-gates left of the field-gate. The track leads unerringly by three field-gates to the end of Hundreds Lane (merging from the left). Keep forward along the continuing Robin Lane, gently descending into Troutbeck, arriving beside the village institute and post office, now a most welcome café - here's to it being still open!

20d Follow the village street north; watch for St John's Well, set into the left-hand wall, and after this find a lane bearing right by Myley Ghyll - this is the Roman road. The lane becomes a narrow footpath before

Troutbeck bank-barn

opening upon a road. Keep forward with this and carefully cross the A592, entering the continuing narrow footpath signed 'Ing Lane' to merge with the narrow road. Go right with Ing Lane, crossing Ing Bridge and, after a gate, Hagg Bridge.

20e A footpath is signposted now, half-right across the pasture, rising to a kissing-gate to join the farm track originating from Troutbeck Park Farm. The track quickly opens as it swings into the Hagg Gill valley, with Troutbeck Tongue rising sharply to the left - the name a Norse term, with 'hag' referred to the cutting of timber. Can there be any doubt that this track is anything other than the Roman way?

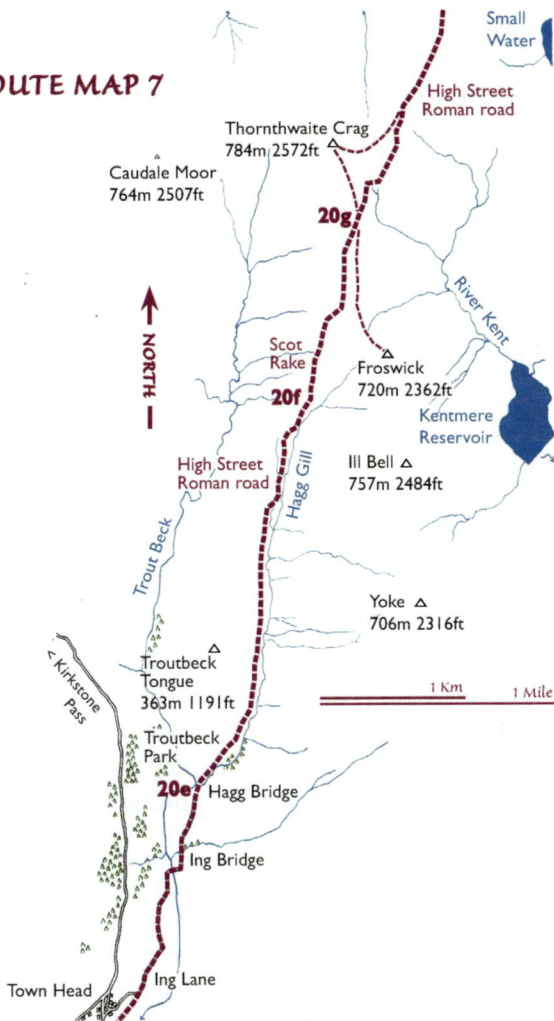

ROUTE MAP 7

Small Water

High Street
Roman road

Thornthwaite Crag
784m 2572ft △

Caudale Moor
764m 2507ft

20g

River Kent

NORTH ↑

Scot
Rake

Froswick
720m 2362ft △

20f

Kentmere
Reservoir

High Street
Roman road

Hagg Gill

Ill Bell △
757m 2484ft

Trout Beck

Yoke △
706m 2316ft

Troutbeck
Tongue
363m 1191ft △

1 Km   1 Mile

< Kirkstone Pass

Troutbeck
Park

20e Hagg Bridge

Ing Bridge

Town Head

Ing Lane

At the first gate, glance down right to see a handsome, tree-shaded clapper bridge over the beck. On the opposite side of the valley runs a parallel track, used by wagons carrying slate from the quarry with its great spoil tips. There is another old quarry a little further up the valley. The track now carries mountain bikers intent on climbing onto High Street by Scot Rake. Spot the sad barn in the valley bottom, its central wall collapsed - the roof cannot but fall in soon!

Two more gates are negotiated and eventually the adjacent wall angles away, setting the track free, which in due course drifts across the shallow bowl at the head of the valley. Notice the great landslip up to the left, one of the many such caused by the outrageous storms in December 2015. The route now rises easily, as a green way comes to a hand-gate.

20f From the hand-gate, step up and climb on, with a wall close to the left and with the bracken held at bay on the grass path by regular use. The views back to the long low ridge of Troutbeck Tongue are intriguing; you can tell by its form that the sculpting Ice Age glacier was travelling south. Neolithic cairns lie on the near plateau of the ridge, indicating an ancient settlement in this area.

Again, the trail loses its wall and runs on up the fell as a loose stony path, coming over a simple rock step to become a grass trod (dialect for 'path') once more. The angle is steep but the pony track, as that is what it looks like, is assured. A small re-entrant gill is slipped through, as the path again turns to climb ever more intently, coming onto the ridge where the popular Kentmere horseshoe trail is met. The modern substrate-inverted path replicates what, in all probability, the Romans will have done in many similarly marshy situations along the spine of the range. The near summit of Froswick is strikingly apparent to the south. One can peer over the edge into the Kentmere valley to spy the reservoir but, as the ridge path climbs on, attention will be drawn far more widely west into the mountain heart of Lakeland.

20g The Roman road breaks from the regular line of ridge walkers, who are primarily intent on reaching Thornthwaite Crag, with its great beacon cairn. This is well off the Roman line. The clue for this is the two wrought-iron fence stakes which indicate a path to the right that clings to the Kentmere edge. Looking back,

Rainsborrow Crag, Ill Bell and Froswick from the Roman road east of Thornthwaite Crag.

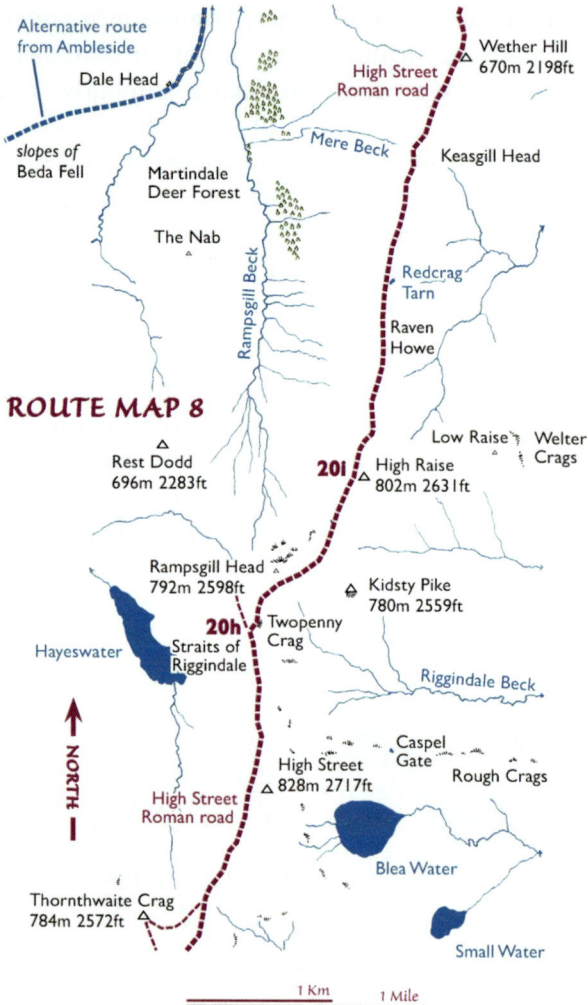

Alternative route
from Ambleside

Dale Head

slopes of
Beda Fell

Martindale
Deer Forest

The Nab

Wether Hill
670m 2198ft

High Street
Roman road

Mere Beck

Keasgill Head

Rampsgill Beck

Redcrag
Tarn

Raven
Howe

ROUTE MAP 8

Rest Dodd
696m 2283ft

Low Raise

Welter
Crags

20l High Raise
802m 2631ft

Rampsgill Head
792m 2598ft

Kidsty Pike
780m 2559ft

20h Twopenny
Crag

Hayeswater

Straits of
Riggindale

Riggindale Beck

Caspel
Gate

High Street
828m 2717ft

Rough Crags

NORTH

High Street
Roman road

Blea Water

Thornthwaite Crag
784m 2572ft

Small Water

1 Km   1 Mile

Froswick is overtopped by the imperiously peaked Ill Bell. The narrow trod slips through a shallow re-entrant, the next more significant gully being a headwater of the River Kent.

Now the possible Roman way leaves the edge, but not flamboyantly. You'll not detect it at this stage, although the actual line can be found by diligent searching, betrayed by the change in vegetation revealing the characteristic 15ft-wide passage; interestingly, it's not used by modern walkers until the popular track from Thornthwaite Crag is met after the peat hags. The wear has left scant evidence except the characteristic width. Through the wall and due north, the ancient ridge way avoids the summit of High Street, though you are not precluded; simply follow the wall.

The old way provides the most perfect promenade and, with fair weather, eyes will be constantly averted west, with the Helvellyn range wonderfully pre-eminent. The trail inclines down to slip through the ridge wall at the enigmatically named Straits of Riggindale, where the ridge tightens to a narrow waist. Here, the view east down the great U-shaped Riggindale is awesome.

20h Climbing beyond, be sure to veer off right at the first opportunity to come over Twopenny Crag and look back at the most stunning view of High Street (as portrayed on the book cover). Alfred Wainwright's hugely popular Coast to Coast Walk, heading for the prominent Kidsty Pike, is briefly joined at this point but, as a rocky crest is met, the Roman way veers half-left with subsequent pasture. You have another opportunity to track down the actual 'road' in the vegetation, invariably identified as a dark brown band not trodden in modern times - that is, until coming over the brow of Rampsgill Head where you begin the ridge descent with High Raise ahead. One gets a fine view into Martindale as you come into the depression. Keep with the obvious path, climbing through the pasture onto High Raise, some 100m west of the rocky summit.

20i Martindale is prominent from the ridge–edge path, which advances to meet a fence from where you get a good long view of the ridge stretching north to Loadpot Hill and the lower reach of Ullswater. You may go through the hand-gate or accompany the fence right to the stile where the ridge wall begins; this is then accompanied on an oft-wet moorland trod over Red Crag (no rocks).

The wall abruptly stops at a fence, with a hand-gate set to its left. After a wet gap, the broken wall resumes and a great pool is passed. The trail passes through the wall and by some large peat hags. A path down into Fusedale effectively follows the wall, should you be looking to break the journey to link with the alternative route from Ambleside in Martindale. Otherwise plod on along the moorland ridge, passing the modest cairn on Wether Hill and descending by more hags and a generous tarn in the depression. Now ascend to Lowther House - the barest footings of a chimneystack remain from an otherwise Victorian timber shooting lodge.

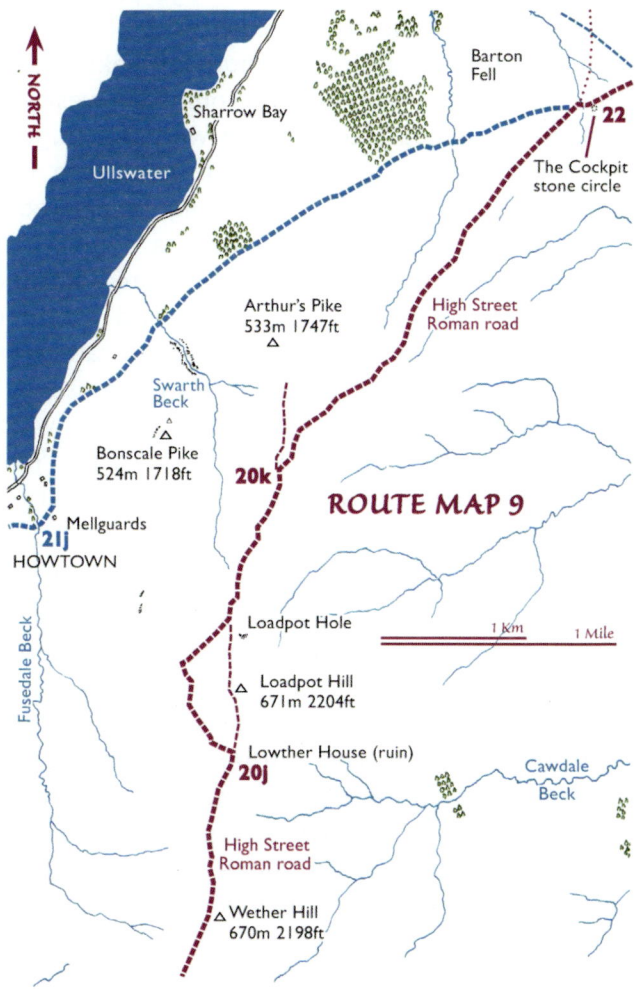

NORTH

Sharrow Bay

Barton Fell

Ullswater

22

The Cockpit
stone circle

Arthur's Pike
533m 1747ft

High Street
Roman road

Swarth
Beck

Bonscale Pike
524m 1718ft

20k

ROUTE MAP 9

Mellguards

21j
HOWTOWN

Fusedale Beck

Loadpot Hole

1 km   1 Mile

Loadpot Hill
671m 2204ft

Lowther House (ruin)

Cawdale
Beck

20j

High Street
Roman road

Wether Hill
670m 2198ft

20j While the natural line of the ridge path heads on over the summit plateau of Loadpot Hill, the actual Roman road weirdly and very tangibly breaks sharp left at this point. Follow suit, coming round the west side of the fell in a great arc to re-unite with the ridge path below Loadpot Hole - thought to have been a Roman roadstone quarry. The fell-name long associated with this hollow suggests it to have been a source of iron ore, but the Roman connection is the more plausible. In the adjacent sunken way you might find a boundary stone known as 'Lambert Lad'. Maps indicate a stone circle over to the left, though in fact three stones can be seen a little below where the map implies, which is odd - Lambert Lad may very well be one such 'moved' stone. The Roman way and the contemporary path head on north.

20k Be sure to take the right-hand fork off the more obvious path towards Arthur's Pike (at grid ref 462198). Never fear if you miss it as the modern way is actually drier and achieves the same objective - the track from Howtown, only a little way west of the Roman intersection. The authentic path can seem interminable, through rough moor grass, heather and marsh, with the worst sponge and rushes inevitably occurring as the slope flattens. Due relief arrives as the track from Howtown is met. Turn right, fording Aik Beck, to reach The Cockpit stone circle.

Ambleside to The Cockpit via Scandale Pass, Boredale Hause and Martindale

The inter-fort march from Ambleside to Brocavum was a mighty 25 miles, no mean undertaking even in our time. The Romans hiked such distances in a day... though YOU don't have to! The journey from Ambleside to Askham can be neatly broken in two (staying overnight in Patterdale) by following a different line over Scandale Pass and Boredale Hause, though you'll be pleased to learn that a short stretch of Roman road is encountered! This 'road' actually crossed Kirkstone Pass, which today has an Inn for refreshment so you may opt to ascend the Stock Ghyll valley as distinct from the route proposed here. However, the Scandale route is altogether more engaging with the fells and completely removed from the dissonance of modern traffic.

21a With your walk objective of Patterdale in mind, break from the primary route at Miller Bridge and bear right to traverse Rothay Park, coming by the impressive modern Parish Centre and the huge Victorian spire of St Mary's church, passing the primary school to meet the street by Zefferelli's. Head up the street and bear left, passing the novel Bridge House and coming to the small roundabout by the Armitt Museum (including a Roman gravestone found near the east gate of the fort).

21b Turn up the steep start to the Kirkstone Road by the Golden Rule public house. Above, glance right to see How Head, the oldest house in the town. Keep with the road until you see Sweden Bridge Lane, indicated

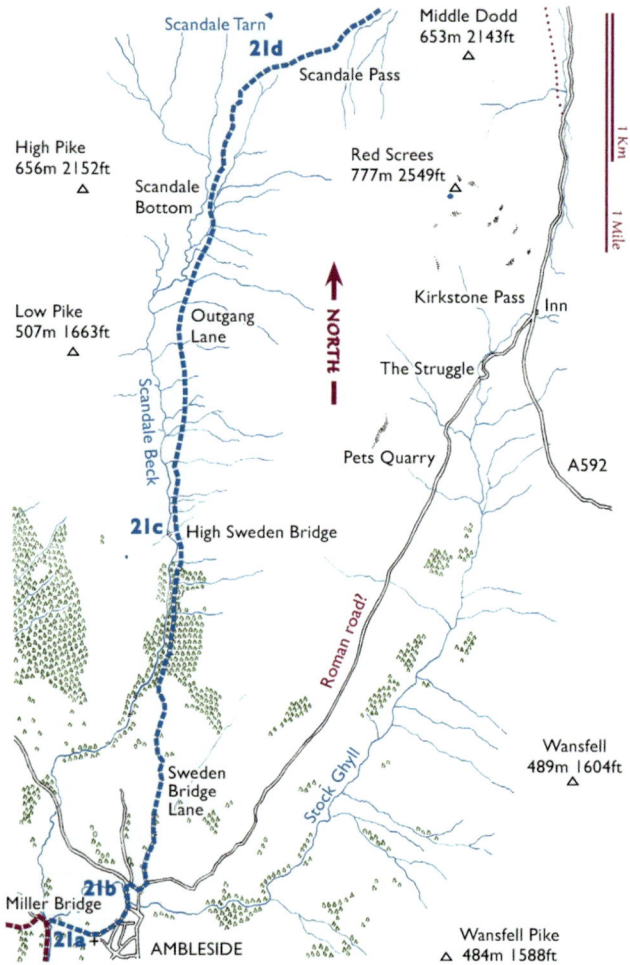

ROUTE MAP 10

Scandale Tarn

2Id

Scandale Pass

Middle Dodd
653m 2143ft
△

High Pike
656m 2152ft
△

Scandale
Bottom

Red Screes
777m 2549ft
△

Low Pike
507m 1663ft
△

Outgang
Lane

NORTH ↑

Kirkstone Pass   Inn

The Struggle

Scandale Beck

Pets Quarry

A592

2Ic High Sweden Bridge

Roman road!

Sweden
Bridge
Lane

Stock Ghyll

Wansfell
489m 1604ft
△

2Ib

Miller Bridge

2Ia +

AMBLESIDE

Wansfell Pike
△ 484m 1588ft

1 Km

1 Mile

44

left. Follow this quiet road and, as adjacent houses end, enter the narrow walled lane. Early on, there are lovely views over the wooded vale. Spot the red sandstone gate posts with metal hand-gates, which betray the unseen passage of the Thirlmere Aqueduct to Manchester and, on the right, a traditional gate stoup with hazel stakes.

After this point the views become ever more impressive over the wooded vale to nearer fells and the great heights of Coniston and Great Langdale. The lane leads by the standing wall of an old barn and a gate at the top of Sweden Wood to pass through a gate. A few paces on, spot a fallen tree festooned with coins! Then, after passing two deep, dark slate quarries, go through another gate and arrive at a path junction. Close by, down to the left, see the enchanting High Sweden Bridge, a popular spot for creative cameras.

21c Keep to the main track, which soon becomes the walled outgang lane. A hugely attractive undulating passage leads into the upper dale, with several minor gills to ford. Scandale means 'short valley'. Ending at a gate, note how the upper bowl of the mountain valley is a mass of young tree sheaths, promising a verdant future for this lovely dalehead. Coming by a compound sheepfold, go through a gate and begin the easy ascent to Scandale Pass. Initially flanked by bracken, the regular way opens into a really pleasing fell trail to reach and cross the ladder-stile at Scandale Pass.

21d This saddle in the ridge connects Red Screes (east), which imperiously overbears Kirkstone Pass, with the shapely top of Little Hart Crag (west). The descent into Caiston Glen is of a different character to the grassy rise from Scandale. The fell path is steeper and has some rocky ground, requiring a steady pace. Spot the spoil from an old lead mine on the far bank, close by a lovely cascade. Soon the path has a wall close on the right which leads to a fold enclosure - pass through via hand-gates.

The path heads on through lightly wooded pasture, passing a low outbarn and mature pollarded ash to go to the right of a large field-barn via a hand-gate, where you enter a large enclosure dotted with huge stones. These glacial erratics look like a mammoth's stone circle. In fact, this area contained the medieval township of High Hartsop, itself resting upon a Roman settlement, as there was a Roman road coming through the site from Kirkstone Pass.

Brotherswater from just above Boredale Hause

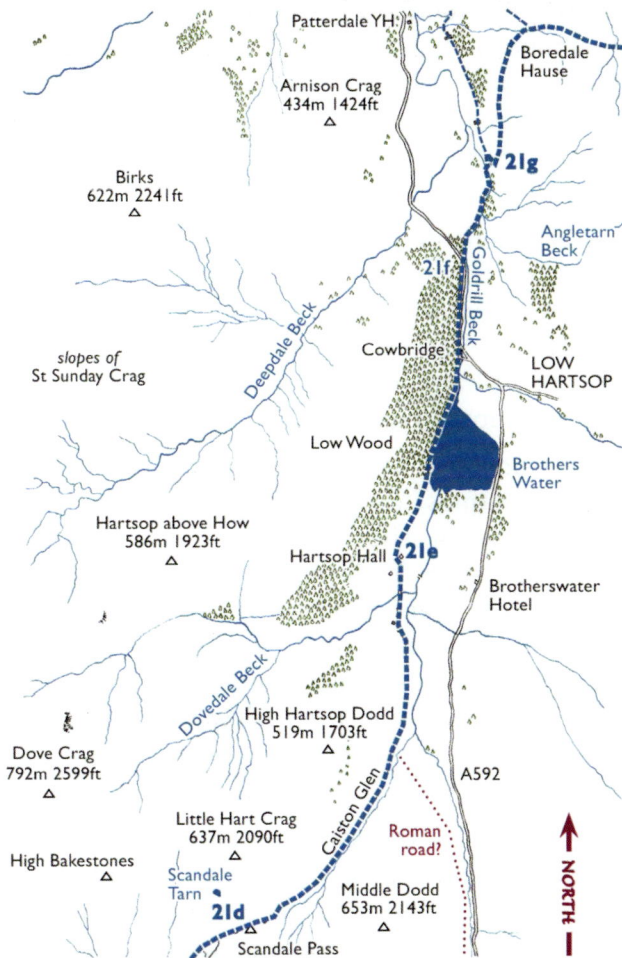

ROUTE MAP 11

1 Km 1 Mile

Patterdale YH

Boredale Hause

Arnison Crag
434m 1424ft

21g

Angletarn
Beck

Birks
622m 2241ft

Goldrill Beck

21f

Cowbridge

LOW
HARTSOP

slopes of
St Sunday Crag

Deepdale Beck

Low Wood

Brothers
Water

Hartsop above How
586m 1923ft

Hartsop Hall

21e

Brotherswater
Hotel

Dovedale Beck

High Hartsop Dodd
519m 1703ft

Dove Crag
792m 2599ft

Caiston Glen

A592

Little Hart Crag
637m 2090ft

Roman
road?

High Bakestones

Scandale
Tarn

Middle Dodd
653m 2143ft

21d

Scandale Pass

NORTH

47

The continuing footpath now joins that Roman way, crossing a wooden bridge. The ensuing track aims for barns, but the footpath takes the right-hand fork after 50m, aiming for a hand-gate in the wall. Pass to the left of Hartsop Hall - though you may relish the knowledge that Brotherswater Inn and Sykeside campsite can swiftly be reached along the farm access track to the east.

21e After two hand-gates, the open track (and therefore Roman road) comes beside Brotherswater, in a beautiful canopy of native woodland. Meeting the hand-gate into Cowbridge car park, don't go through but instead veer left by the wall and embark on an undulating permitted footpath (National Trust sign, 'to Patterdale').

21f The woodland path comes to a kissing-gate from where, with utmost care, cross the A592 and hop over the fence-stile. A short woodland way leads beside Goldrill Beck, soon following the top of the flood bank via two stiles to reach a bridge, where a farm track from Deepdale Bridge crosses the beck. Follow suit, rising by a gate. To reach Patterdale, a little over one mile away, simply keep forward on the trackway by gates through Beckstones and Crookabeck to Rooking, where you turn left on the main road.

When returning to the trail the following day, in effect bear right to find a gate waymarked 'Boredale Hause', gaining access to the steep inclining bridle-path.

21g The primary route takes the acute right-hand turn and promptly goes through a second gate. After 250 yards, you'll come upon the course of the old

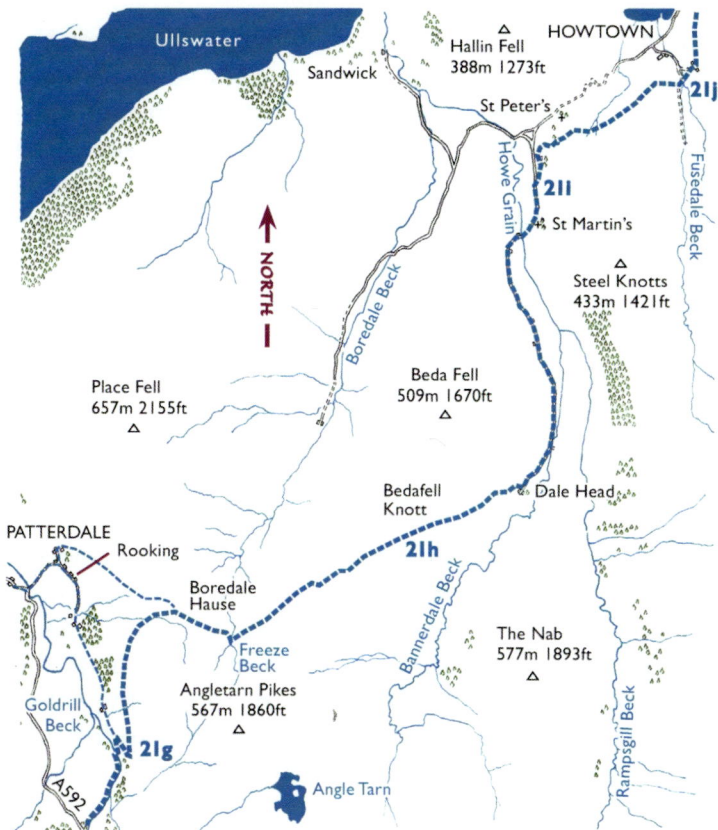

ROUTE MAP 12

Ullswater

1 Km
1 Mile

Hallin Fell
388m 1273ft

HOWTOWN

Sandwick

St Peter's

21j

Howe Grain

21i

St Martin's

Fusedale Beck

NORTH

Boredale Beck

Steel Knotts
433m 1421ft

Place Fell
657m 2155ft

Beda Fell
509m 1670ft

Bedafell
Knott

Dale Head

PATTERDALE

Rooking

Boredale
Hause

21h

Bannerdale Beck

The Nab
577m 1893ft

Freeze
Beck

Angletarn Pikes
567m 1860ft

Goldrill
Beck

21g

A592

Angle Tarn

Rampsgill Beck

49

Hayeswater Aqueduct and switch acutely left with it (the pipe set under the rough path), climbing quite steeply and passing a trackside tank to merge with the path direct from Patterdale, via Rooking.

Keep walking east, a brief marshy patch may cause the path to become confused, but the path soon resumes bearing south-east and, rising, slips through the shallow re-entrant of Freeze Beck, and runs along the brink of a steep slope in a groove to cross the ridge between Angletarn Pikes and Bedafell Knott. From here the High Street skyline is hugely impressive, traversed by the Roman road and therefore the primary route of Hadrian's High Way.

21h The bridle-path now dips over the edge, peering into the lonely crag-rimmed Bannerdale, with its handsome view of The Nab and Rest Dodd, the heart of Martindale Deer Forest. The trail kinks by a ruin and continues to angle down, latterly brushing bracken and gaining a bird's eye view into the dale bottom, where the resident herd of wild red deer can often be seen grazing. The green sward path leads through a field-gate and comes above Dale Head Farm. Go through the gate, into and through the farmyard, to join the valley road. Keep with the road, crossing Christy Bridge and running on by the charming church of St Martin, rebuilt in 1633 with Quakerish simplicity.

21i Watch for the footpath off the road on the right, signed 'The Coombs'. From the gate, a greenway proceeds - in all probability this was the original valley road to Howtown. The path skirts round by Cotehow,

The Roman road approaching the Straits of Riggindale on the slopes of High Street

formerly the Star Inn. Ignore the accessing track and keep up beside the wall along the top of the bank, passing a scenic seat to come round to a metal gate. Go left, passing the rush-filled Lanty Tarn and keep right, striding on down the green path, now with Ullswater's lower reach in open view. The path steps onto the open road in Fusedale, over the cattle grid to reach the Howtown Hotel with its café.

21j However, the trail heeds the stand-alone bridleway sign 'Swarthbeck' and goes down to cross the clapper bridge, leading into the walled funnel to a gate to join the road, leading to the prominent white house, Mellguards. Beyond the front door, go through the inviting gate and join the track that now runs on

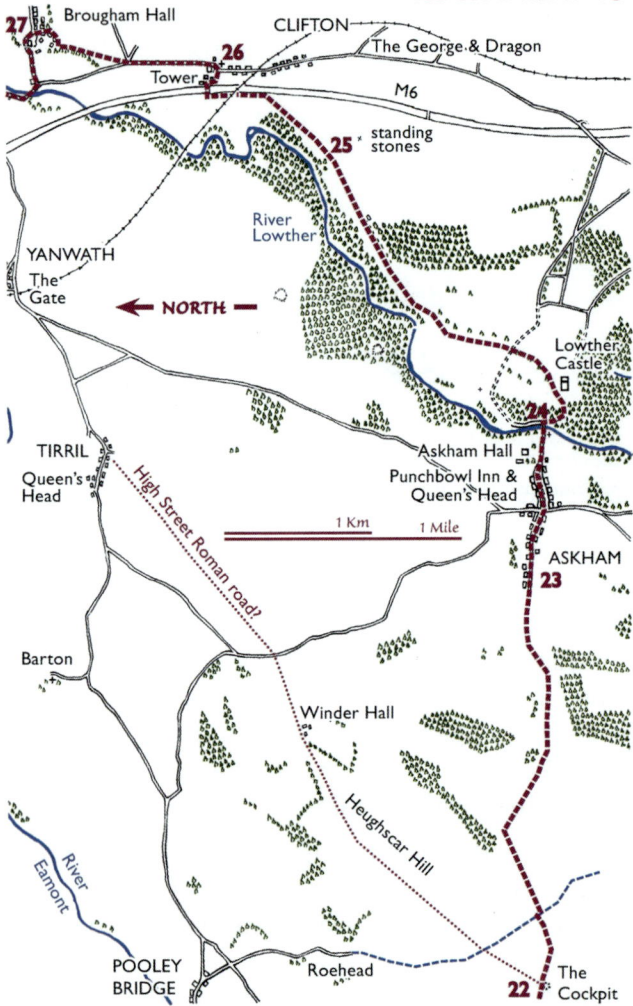

27

Brougham Hall

CLIFTON

The George & Dragon

26

Tower

M6

25

standing
stones

River
Lowther

YANWATH

The
Gate

← NORTH →

Lowther
Castle

24

TIRRIL

Queen's
Head

Askham Hall

Punchbowl Inn &
Queen's Head

High Street Roman road?

1 Km   1 Mile

ASKHAM

23

Barton

Winder Hall

Heughscar Hill

River
Eamont

POOLEY
BRIDGE

Roehead

22

The
Cockpit

unhindered, below the great scarp of Bonscale and Arthur's Pike, en route crossing a footbridge over Swarth Beck, gradually gaining height and, within two miles, arrives upon The Cockpit stone circle, uniting with High Street Roman road and Hadrian's High Way.

22 Evidently once a place of illicit blood sport, it's now a lovely spot to stand, stare and consider the long passage of time that this site evokes. The Roman road breaks half-left from The Cockpit, striking over Heughscar Hill and heading for Tirril - not a route that is taken on the High Way, though you may choose to go that way.

The more inspiring walking option focuses on reaching Brougham via Askham, Lowther and Clifton. Keep with the primary made path from the stone circle, which aims slightly north of east to a staggered crossing of the green way between Roehead and Helton. Head up the facing turf way towards the corner of the skyline woodland. Coming by a small cairn, drift naturally right with the gentle scarp, looking towards the towers of Lowther Castle, tucked into the woods above Askham. The grassy way comes down to a broad field-gate and carries on as a clear trackway, joining a road advancing by a cattle grid into Askham Townhead.

23 The village road runs on down to arrive at The Queens Head and Askham Stores/café, welcome sights for sure! Further down the beautifully open, green-lined street, gorgeously graced with delightful 17th and 18th century cottages, you'll also find the Punchbowl Inn and Askham Hall Hotel with its café. Lurking behind the

Askham Hall's impressive south facade

hall's grand 18th-century frontage is a 15th-century defended tower from the pillaging age of the Border Reiver. The route continues down the road, past the church, to cross the River Lowther.

24 At once turn right and take the rising path in the woodland to come upon the corner wall of Lowther Castle's ornamental grounds, whose former imposing glories are suggested by the Doric doorway. Cross the cattle-grid and follow the open track, which sweeps past the grand façade of Lowther Castle, progressively undergoing a revitalising facelift after long years of sad neglect. There is a café in the courtyard, should you wish to visit. The route, however, continues upon the main track, sweeping down the avenue of trees to cross the public road. Where the main track veers left, go straight on with the lesser track, leading through pasture gates and passing Buckholme Lodge.

25 The next gate is equipped with a stile. From this point you may be interested to visit two standing stones, 300m distant and reached by the footpath that breaks right into a farm track from this point. The High Way, however, keeps to the track ahead, becoming enclosed. Coming by the M6 motorway, it turns sharp left and passes under the West Coast mainline, rising to cross Clifton Hall Bridge. At hand is the sturdy Clifton Hall Tower, in the care of English Heritage, where you may climb the stairs and marvel at the interior structure, especially the timbers. It dates from the 15th century and, for all its castle-like appearance, was not defensive, since it was the tower end of the original farmhouse - you can see the faint impression of its roofline in the south wall.

Take heed: the footpath does not go boldly on through the farmyard! Instead, it is ushered round the near right barn from a metal kissing-gate, goes via a stile and gates by the horse paddock, then up the field to a wall-stile onto the A6, opposite St Cuthbert's - the parish church of Clifton, set prominently on a mound. Clifton's place in history might be said to have been of a day's duration, when the bedraggled remnants of the retreating Jacobite Rebellion army were set upon by the troops of the Duke of Cumberland in 1745.

26 Go left, with the roadside footway leading out of the village, passing a roadside bank barn. At the road junction, angle over to the metal-gated doorway in the

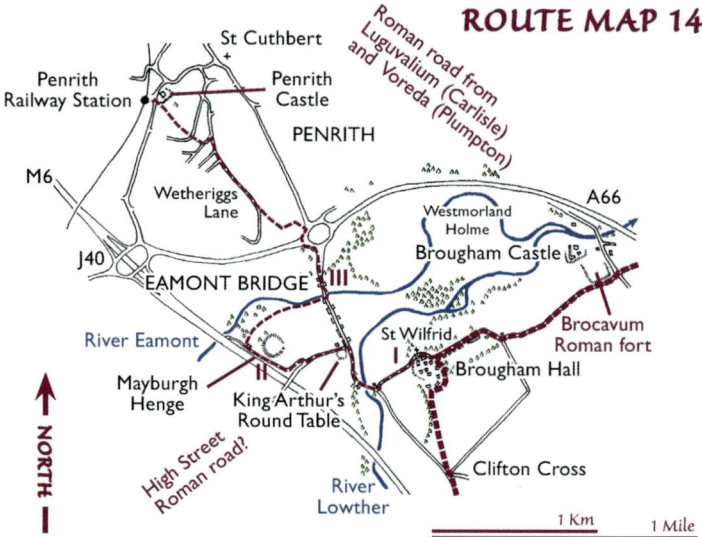

ROUTE MAP 14

St Cuthbert

Penrith Railway Station

Penrith Castle

PENRITH

Roman road from Luguvalium (Carlisle) and Voreda (Plumpton)

M6

Wetheriggs Lane

A66

Westmorland Holme

Brougham Castle

J40

EAMONT BRIDGE

III

River Eamont

Mayburgh Henge

King Arthur's Round Table

II

St Wilfrid

I

Brougham Hall

Brocavum Roman fort

High Street Roman road?

River Lowther

Clifton Cross

NORTH

1 Km   1 Mile

Eamont Bridge

wall, which is the footpath to Brougham Hall. It traverses the field (often under crops) and comes by woodland to reach a fence-stile, entering a tight footpath passage at the edge of private gardens. This leads round and, by a nifty hinged gate-stile, sneaks into the corner of a garden before stepping onto the road in front of the grand door of Brougham Hall. You should take the opportunity to enter, as there is a café in the large courtyard, amongst a range of artisan businesses, including Eden Brewery.

This is the pivot point on Hadrian's High Way. Not quite halfway, but effectively so, given the closeness of the West Coast mainline station at Penrith. This enables the journey to be broken into two superb week-long walking holidays.

The 2.5-mile journey to the railway station is entertaining, and includes several heritage features of considerable importance.

I From the Brougham Hall entrance door head west, taking a moment to admire the door knocker on the original front door, which is a facsimile of the famous dragon's head knocker on Durham Cathedral. Pass under the bridge, which was an access from the hall to the little parish church of St Wilfrid. Follow the road and use its old line by the lodge on a path to reach the A6 footway and bridge over the River Lowther. See the Lowther lodge on the left, a mini replica of the Castle. At the road junction go left, noting the South African memorial on the facing field corner. Given time, go through the kissing-gate to inspect King Arthur's Round

Table - the name is fictitious, the monument not. This is a ceremonial site, some four thousand years old, that begs far more questions than can be answered, though it must have been intertwined with Mayburgh. Continue with the footway to reach the Millennium Stone - installed as a unifying statement of the faiths of Eden - and from here bear down the side road, signed to Southwaite Green Mill.

II   Another kissing-gate invites access to inspect Mayburgh Henge, a great doughnut-shaped ringwork, with a solitary standing stone in its midst - once there was a circle of eight. The henge, a cathedral of its age, is composed of beckstone carried by pilgrims, probably the accumulation of many centuries. The road passes Southwaite Green cottages, seeking a footpath signed right, which leads through to the Bleach Green access drive. Follow the river downstream to the handsome Eamont Bridge, the one survivor from the floods of December 2015 that washed away the grand Pooley Bridge and rendered Brougham Castle Bridge unsafe. There are two pubs in the village as further lure.

III If time is pressing, cross the road at the traffic lights and the metal footbridge ascending Kemplay Bank. Cross the broad busy road near the top where KEEP CLEAR is painted on the road. Pass in front of the old toll bar bungalow to reach the pedestrian crossing, using the lights on a very busy traffic roundabout junction. Follow the footway on round by the roundabout to enter the confined footpath leading to the suburban street, Wetheriggs Lane. Keep forward, passing the cricket club and Ullswater School, after the next road junction from the right, and coming to the rear of the Sainsbury's car park, turn left with Castle Hill Road. Veer right with the first cul-de-sac. Follow the path up a brief bank and cross an intervening road, continuing by the fence-confined path into Castle Park. Keep straight on, rounding the pavilion and following the tree avenue, with Penrith Castle close on the right. Go through the arched entrance and, over the busy road, arrive directly upon the station forecourt.

~

Thus concludes part one of Hadrian's High Way. This epic journey continues in part two, a separate guide book taking the intrepid follower of the High Way from Brougham Castle to Bardon Mill, just below Hadrian's eponymous wall.

As with part one, the traveller has options to avoid inhospitable countryside in the event of foul weather.

Heading from Brougham Castle, south of Penrith, the route visits Ninekirks and wends by the Eden to Kirkby Thore and so by Milburn to follow the Roman Maiden Way over the high Pennine watershed to the Epiacum Roman fort near Alston.

Now in the South Tyne valley it ventures north, still in harmony with the Roman road to reach Greenhead. Arriving upon the Roman Wall, the final leg explores the high Whin Sill section of the frontier to Housesteads, cutting back to the magnificent Roman excavations at Vindolanda and concluding at the Bardon Mill railway station.

NOTES

NOTES